Japanese Zen Gardens

Russell Chard

Welcome to 'Japanese Zen Gardens ' a book that will bring to life these extraordinary art forms.

Zen gardens are gardens that are steeped in hundreds of years of history and tradition together with, in many cases, a significant religious influence. Whether you have visited a Japanese style garden or not, you will certainly find the information in this publication interesting, helpful and inspiring. They can be very small and sit on a table-top all the way through to much larger space gardens which means there is an appropriate Zen garden for everyone's tastes, space and budgets.

This book is all about ZEN gardens ,detailing their history, meaning, influence and stunning simplicity. A Zen style garden is becoming increasingly desirable and is more than ever at the popular end of garden design. Purists would be regimented in its design and elements but we all have choice and freewill as part of our lives and it by no means a sin to create a garden in a Zen style rather than a one hundred per cent authentic garden.

In addition to all that I have mentioned already, this edition contains specific design tips and instructions on how to simply build a Zen garden in your home with instructions and pictures and the good news is it is nowhere near as daunting as you may think.

In a world full of stress and angst there is nowhere better to relax and contemplate than in a Zen garden and your friends and family will be seriously impressed with your efforts!

You may wish to consider an adaptation of a Zen garden known as a 'Courtyard ' garden an incarnation of Japanese gardens that dates back to the 14th century and that today occupy some of the worlds 'coolest' homes and public buildings. Discover their facets and meaning with us.

Irrespective of whether you wish to design a garden or not, the answer to the question 'What is a Zen garden?' is all here in simple plain English. Over 150,000 people worldwide search for that specific term on Google every month……the answer is right here! Enjoy.

  Russell Chard – ***Publisher 'Japanese and Zen Gardens***

Related websites:
www.makingajapanesegarden.com
www.japzen.wordpress.com
www.japzengardens.org

 facebook.com/japanesegardens

 @japangdninfo

Copyright © 2013 by Zenibo Publishing

All rights reserved. No part of this book may be reproduced in any form or by any electronic or mechanical means including information storage and retrieval systems – except in the case of brief quotations in articles or reviews – without the permission in writing from its publisher, Zenibo Publishing

All brand names and product names used in this book are trademarks, registered trademarks, or trade names of their respective holders. We are not associated with any product or vendor in this book.

Contents

A History of Zen Gardens   7

The Meaning of Zen Gardens   13

Types of Zen Gardens   21

Ingredients of Zen Gardens   27

Making Your Own Zen Garden:
   What You Need to Know   35

Building a Small Zen Garden   44

Making a Japanese Courtyard Garden   55

A HISTORY OF ZEN GARDENS

Whether you're aware of what a Zen Garden is or not, you have most likely seen one – a tranquil harmonious place with rocks, sand or gravel and manicured plants and shrubs is probably the most renowned imagery of a Zen Garden. These picturesque gardens, ideal for meditating or simply viewing, are seen enwreathing most religious edifices in Japan, like the famous Buddhist temples in Kyoto.

Zen Gardens are characterized as such because of the calmness they invoke, which is what makes them ideal for meditation, reflection and relaxation. Inspired initially by Buddhism and Chinese culture, the word ZEN would be written on soil and sand, which is the root and inspiration of Zen Gardens. But a Zen Garden should have more than one meaning for the viewer. As the Japanese say, "the mind is flexible if we practice flexibility", thus each garden bears its own interpretation.

But before we elaborate on what a Zen Garden is, means and what comprises it, let's first take a journey to the past and unearth the roots and derivation of these beautiful gardens.

Each period marks its own significant point in the rise, enhancement and adaptation of Zen Gardens in the Japanese culture.

These periods are:

- The Han Dynasty
- The Asuka Era
- The Nara Era
- The Heian Era
- The Kamakura Era

THE HAN DYNASTY

Although the aspect of Zen Gardens is associated with Japan, it is historically accepted as being a tradition imported from China during what is known as the Han Dynasty (206 – 220 BCE). This recreation, which was more of a philosophy, was adopted by the Japanese and enhanced to their culture. This is why Japanese gardens exemplify a "lighter" version of Chinese ones and generally follow fewer aesthetic rules and design guidelines in the creation process.

The first Zen Garden was created by Chinese Emperor Wu Di, who lived from 140-87 BCE. This garden depicted three small islands and it eventually became a custom to use rocks and greenery in order to form island-like motifs and mimic nature. These particular islands were meant to represent the Isles of the Immortals or Taoist gods, a trend that would be replicated throughout the years.

However, the aspects represented in the gardens of the Han Dynasty period were based on imaginary places, godly realms and mythological landscapes. This imitation of imaginary places went on until the early 600s AD, when the first nature-inspired hill and pond garden was created in Japan by Chinese Emperor Yang Di, who enjoyed good relations with the country.

The Emperor's overtures were enticing enough for the Japanese to send their own envoy to China - a man called Ono no Imoko. Imoko who immersed himself in Chinese culture and upon his return to Japan brought all that he had learnt with him, including the art of gardening and Buddhism.

THE ASUKA ERA

During the Asuka period (estimated at 538-710 AD) a new philosophy and religion began to emerge, known as Shinto. Shinto, meaning "Way of the Gods" in Chinese, was a religion that looked upon nature as a god(s), which is what led to the open worship of certain types of rocks and trees.

When a certain "deity" rock was used, sealed by a rice straw rope, in order to indicate an area as being sacred, then that was basically a Zen Garden of the Asuka Era. The Japanese word niwa was a term often used to determine the holy piece of land around a stone or tree, a dominant aspect of Shinto Zen gardening, particularly between 552-646 AD.

THE NARA ERA

The Nara Era (710-794 AD) accentuates the blend of Chinese and Japanese culture, Chinese-influenced garden architecture being one of many examples. A strong characteristic of gardens during this period were the Shinden, which revolved around the element of walkways; paths that connected buildings to each other, with stones and shrubs complimenting the buildings themselves. Shinden gardens

would usually adorn royal edifices or temples and shrines.

With teachings like Buddhism and Shinto broadly introduced to the Japanese culture, the gardens fashioned in this period would be looked upon as depictions of the cosmos. A large stone would be placed in the centre of them in order to indicate the home of the Buddha and the centre of the universe. Encircling that stone, smaller ones would be placed in representation of the Buddha's disciples.

THE HEIAN ERA

From 794 to 1185AD, otherwise known as the Heian Era, the Japanese culture was defined by elegance and luxury. This period of opulence in Japan was in which gardens too developed a more luxurious feel to them and were thus usually the domains of wealthier people. Zen Gardens suddenly became status symbols indicating wealth and reputation. These rich land-owners were expected to be connoisseurs of Zen Gardens according to the newly developed rules.

It is in the Heian period that we see boats floating upon

garden ponds, another advantage that applied to the owners of these lavish gardens. These gardens were specifically known as Chisen Shuyu Teien, translating as "Pond-spring boating gardens" in English. Ponds would essentially be the epicentre of such a garden as well as the spot from which one would view the garden as a whole. Taking a tranquil boat-ride through the pond was the traditional way of viewing the garden and a method of entertaining guests.

What we refer to today as Modern Japanese Gardening actually stems from the Heian Era. Sakuteiki, the first book ever written on Japanese gardening and that dates back to the 11th century, was written by Tachibana Toshitsuna, whose father Fujiwara Yorimichi ruled Japan for nearly half a century and was also the renowned builder of the in Kyoto. The Sakuteiki, or "Book of Gardens", indicated the starting point of Japanese gardening and was also the book that freed designers from the constraints of Chinese-influenced gardening in Japan, which was strictly based on Feng Shui principles and geometric rules. What the Sakuteiki recommended was a breakthrough in this rule, suggesting that the garden designer should use the placement of stones as their number one priority.

THE KAMAKURA ERA

The Kamakura Era ran between 1185-1392 and was a period of great change in Japanese garden design due to the Zen influence. The new Shogun and his Samurai had embraced the Zen religion, thus influencing the role and purpose of Japanese gardens, which evolved into meditational grounds.

This is where the label "Zen Gardens" firstly and officially applies. Now that the gardens were enhanced for religious purposes, the designers behind them would largely be priests and sometimes even designers with religious affiliations. The priests were known as Ishitateso (rock setting priests) and were younger, lesser-ranked priests; elders would consider such work as beneath them.

One of the leading garden designers during the Kamakura Era was Muso Soseki (1275-1351), also known as the forefather of "Borrowed Scenery". Soseki designed the gardens in such a way, that the visitor would actually walk around the garden to view it as opposed to sitting in a boat or looking from a building. The idea was that the visitor would think about the changing views of the garden as they moved around it. Soseki's design principle, also called "Hide and Reveal" in Japanese, is evident in some Japanese garden designs to this day.

THE MEANING OF ZEN GARDENS

The beauty of Zen Gardens has transcended through a consequence of eras and is still part of, not only Japanese, but our universal culture today. It has adapted to multiple styles and interpretations, evolving throughout the ages. But what is the core meaning of Zen Gardens? What do they symbolize and represent? And what are those elements that distinguish a Zen Garden from an average garden?

ZEN GARDEN PRINCIPLES

Simplicity is the word that captures all the essence of a Zen Garden's design. While average Western gardens tend to be packed with adornments until no further space is available, a Zen Garden evokes a constant tribute to minimalism. Less is, after all, more in the Japanese culture. Tidiness, precision and an informal, natural character are also what make a Zen Garden true to its cause.

The rules of Zen gardens state that the top two requirements are purity and minimalism (restraint); no single feature should dominate the garden, it is though a personal decision as to whether you wish to have a Zen garden or stretch this mantra and have a garden of Zen influence.

Early Japanese gardens imitated natural landscapes and took inspiration from Japanese landscape painters who had a very strong influence over garden design in the late 14th and early 15th century.

As far back as the 13th century the seven aspects of Zen were determined and defined as follows:

1. Nature and naturalness
2. Simplicity
3. Asymmetry
4. Minimalist sublimity
5. Tranquillity
6. Subtle profoundness
7. Freedom from attachment

Extravagantly decorated Western gardens can appear cluttered to look at but with a minimal Zen Garden the actual art-form aims to not over-stimulate the mind; essentially, the Zen Garden is there to output peace and serenity while evoking tranquil contemplation.

A Zen Garden should be planned with the "spirit" of Zen in mind. The setting should be quiet and peaceful, bright colours should be avoided and landscaping and planting should be kept to a minimum.

ZEN GARDEN DESIGN

Three basic principles apply to a Zen Garden's design:

1. Reduced Scale
2. Symbolization
3. Shakkei ("Borrowed Scenery")

Reduced Scale is one of the key principles of making a Zen Garden. The size of a regular garden would be reduced to basically a miniature, as Zen Gardens aim to represent and symbolize nature minimally, not over-accentuate it. This is the very reason that you may have seen table top Zen gardens right the way through to gardens that occupy a large outdoor space. Even a large garden can be an accurate miniaturisation of a real landscape.

Symbolization is another focal element of Zen Garden design and is what makes these gardens so unique. Zen Gardens, though once symbolizing imaginary realms, now basically represent natural scenery in confined spaces. Mountains and islands are replicated with the use of rocks and streams and rivers are imitated with the use of raked sand, when water is not present. Representing nature and depicting its elements via basic, minimal structures is what all Zen Gardens symbolize.

Shakkei or "Borrowed Scenery" is a term first presented in the Sakuteiki during the Heian Era and is the art of incorporating natural existing backgrounds to supplement and compliment the garden. "Borrowed Scenery", giving justice to its name, uses the surrounding plants and scenery to mimic real-life landscapes but on a much smaller, confined scale.

Key Elements of a Zen Garden and their Representations

The essential elements of every Zen Garden are:

- Water
- Stones/Rocks
- Sand/ or Gravel ("dry water")
- Natural Plants
- Ornaments (not mandatory)

We will be elaborating on each element in the chapter on Ingredients. For now, let's take a look at the core meaning and symbolism of each element:

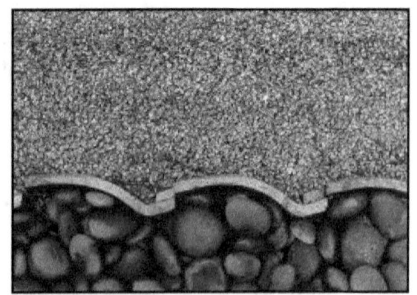

Water symbolizes and represents real-life rivers, seas and streams.

Stones/Rocks depict mythical or natural land forms, mountains or islands. Smaller stones can simply be used as stepping stones and pathways, which symbolize the journey through life.

Sand, or "dry water", symbolizes and mimics water and flow, when water itself is not present. White gravel is also referred to as sand.

Natural Plants have a dual role in Zen Gardens. Small shrubbery can represent trees on a smaller scale, while larger plants can cater as Shakkei.

Ornaments, which are usually objects like lanterns or statues, aren't simply decorative to a Japanese Zen Garden, as they can contribute to the Zen aesthetic as well as Feng Shui harmony of the garden.

BUDDHISM ELEMENTS

As noted in our first chapter, the Japanese culture was introduced to the first elements of Buddhism in the Nara Era. This is clearly depicted in the rocks used in gardens back then to signify the Buddha's domain. Some Zen gardens  also demonstrate the forces of YIN and YANG – the Chinese understanding of natural forces that alter our lives and are responsible for the changes in our environment. In Buddhism a similar belief is called NIYAMAS – a belief of natural forces that can change our lives and world.

Zen Buddhism within a Zen garden dictates that a space must be set aside for its beauty and for ease of meditation. It encourages an area to be allocated for feeding birds and local wildlife. In larger scale Zen gardens paths are numerous and walking them whilst meditating is a natural thing to do. The meditation characteristic was largely assimilated by the gardens of the Kamakura Era which were designed by members of the priesthood. This is one of the greater meanings of Zen Gardens and the philosophy that encompasses them.

Here are some Buddhist gardens around the world that are well worth visiting:

- The Imperial War Museum Peace Garden in London
- Totekiko Temple Gardens in Kyoto, Japan
- The Secret Buddha Garden in Ko Samui, Thailand
- The Peace Pagoda and Peace Temple Gardens in Milton Keynes, UK
- Wenshu Monastery Gardens in Chengdu, China
- Ryoan-ji Temple Gardens –The Temple from the Peaceful Dragon in Kyoto, Japan
- Kagyu Samy Ling Monastery in Scotland

TYPES OF ZEN GARDENS

Zen Gardens consist of a plethora of styles and motifs, each adhering to its own purpose, structure and symbolism. Here are the most popular styles of Zen Gardens:

TEA GARDENS (CHA NIWA OR ROJI)

While the name may suggest an area in which tea can be served, Tea Gardens or Cha Niwa actually cater as passageways to the Tea House or the area in which a Tea Ceremony is conducted. A stroll through the Tea Garden, which connects the outer world to the inner sanctum, aims to calm and relax the guest with its serene surroundings, allowing him/her to release any stress they may be carrying from the outer world before participating in the ceremony.

Tea Gardens are usually small, either stand-alone or connected gardens, and contain ornaments such as Japanese lanterns (toro), a stepping stones (tobi shi), a crouching water basin (tsukubai) and a waiting area (machi-ai). A path (Roji) leads from the entrance of the garden to the Tea House and means "Dewy Path". Water is another element often utilized in Tea Gardens to reflect clean surroundings.

Strolling/Hill Gardens (Tsukiyama)

Strolling Gardens, also known as Tsukiyama or Hill Gardens, as they usually contain an artificial hill in their centre, are the oldest of all Japanese Zen Gardens. Dating back to the Edo era, Tsukiyama Gardens often replicate existing or imaginary landscapes on a smaller scale. These gardens are found in all shapes and sizes and are exquisitely beautiful, featuring elements such as ponds, trees, hills, flowers, stepping stones, bridges and water.

A Strolling or Hill Garden's core purpose is exactly what the name implies; to create a pleasant, serene atmosphere for the guest who opts to walk through it. It is fashioned in such a way that the path through it offers multiple views and aspects of the garden. Famous examples of Hill Gardens can be seen in Kyoto (like the Katsura Rikyu) which are usually viewed from temples. Another form of Hill Gardens is the Kaiyu-Shikien, usually available to the public eye around the world.

Courtyard Gardens (Tsubo Niwa)

Courtyard Gardens or Tsubo Niwa are probably the most versatile Zen Gardens, not to mention one of the most popular. Initially based on the principles of Tea Gardens, these gardens used to belong to rich merchants and landowners and were particularly renowned throughout the 15th century. Today, Courtyard Gardens have enhanced a more contemporary appeal. Since they are generally small, Courtyard Gardens can be placed both outdoors and indoors, which is what makes them so appealing and easy to maintain.

Contemporary small spaces such as rooftops, narrow pathways or passages between buildings and terraces are ideal for these small Courtyard Gardens.

Despite their similarities, Courtyard Gardens are shadier than Tea Gardens, and shade tolerant plants are used. But plants aren't always present in Courtyard Gardens in the modern world, as they can simply be made up of sand, pebbles and rocks.

Dry Landscape Gardens (Karesansui)

Karesansui Gardens are waterless gardens or dry landscape gardens. This style first appeared in the Muromachi period (1333-1568) and draws intense influence and symbolism from Zen ideology and Buddhism, which is why these gardens were essentially placed around the residences (houjou) of Zen abbots.

Core elements to these gardens are rocks, stones and sand. Plants are secondary or simply non-existent in a Karesansui garden and the same applies for water. Raked gravel is used to symbolize trickling streams, rivers and engulfing seas, accompanied by groupings of rocks and stones which usually depict various Chinese mountains. Ryoanji and Daitokuji temples in Kyoto being two famous examples of the Karesansui style. Dry Landscape Gardens are usually viewed from a single, seated perspective.

Flat Gardens (Hiraniwa)

Flat Gardens or Hiraniwa, as implied by the name itself, are the opposite of Hill or Tsukiyama Gardens. Such a design can be implemented in small spaces, which is what makes this gardening style so convenient.

Most temples and buildings with a courtyard front will usually incorporate such a style, as it can cater as a ceremonial ground as well as an ideal meditating area. Gravel paths, simple greenery and sporadic flat stones are what a Hiraniwa garden is essentially all about. This technique allows the guest to be able to appreciate the garden at an open view, without embracing complicated pathways or getting caught in a labyrinth-like garden. Circular patterns, which symbolize happiness and completion, are additionally seen in these gardens and are really quite a trademark.

INGREDIENTS OF ZEN GARDENS

Let's take a look at the significance and symbolism of each ingredient of Zen Gardens separately:

WATER

Streams, ponds and rivers have been excessively used in Zen Gardens throughout the centuries, either in homes or engulfing temples. The reason water is such a vital element to a Zen Garden (as if even represented by sand when not present) is because water is a significant symbol in Zen philosophy and Buddhism, as it interprets clarity, cleanliness and purity – three aspects that cannot be omitted from a meditation garden.

Dripping water in a Zen Garden may signify a measure of time, while rain signifies rebirth. Streaming water is affiliated with life and its course. White gravel (Shirakawa suna or "dry water") depicts oceans in Karesansui gardens, while hand-wash areas are very common in Roji / Tea Gardens. A simple stone basin is used for this purpose.

STONES & ROCKS

Stones and rocks are essential elements to every kind of Zen Garden and are symbolic representations of real or mythical land forms, while this is not their only role. They can also be used as stepping stones, paths, groupings, central stones, and many other types.

The first **Stone Grouping** to be introduced into Japanese gardens was the 'Shumisen' – a collection of stones representing where the Buddha lives (this is placed in the centre of the garden) along with his disciples which are the smaller stones around the Buddha. Centralized traditional Stone Groupings can essentially be called:

    a. The "Buddha Stone" (Mida Buhtsu)

    b. The "Goddess Stone" (Kwannon)

    c. The "Child's Stone" (Seishi)

Yet there are 5 basic types of stone groupings that bear a name, purpose and meaning in Japanese Zen Gardens. These stones and rocks can be used in many combinations.

Positive stones are:

1. The **"Soul Stone"** (Reishoseki), which is low and vertical.
2. The **"Body Stone"** (Taidoseki), which is tall and vertical and always represents a God or person.
3. The **"Heart Stone"** (Shintaiseki) or "Flat Stone" which is flat, as the name implies, and is used as a central stone.
4. The **"Branching Stone"** (Shigyoseki) or "Arching Stone" which has a wider top than base and connects other stones together.
5. The **"Ox Stone"** (Kikyakuseki) or "Reclining Stone" which is always used in conjunction with the Branching Stone.

Negative or bad stones are:

6. **"Diseased Stones"**, which are stones that are withered or have a misshapen top.
7. A **"Dead Stone"**, which is a stone that is a vertical stone used as a horizontal one and vice versa.
8. **"Pauper Stones"**, which are unaffiliated or unconnected to other stones in the garden.

Stones that should NOT be placed in Zen Gardens, as they may affect the Feng Shui element of the garden, are those that are cut, broken or de-formed. Stones moreover shouldn't be placed at right angles to buildings along their axial line and should not be placed near verandas, as this also disrupts the Feng Shui.

Sand

Although a traditional Japanese garden insists on the use of water in its display, contemporary Zen garden owners don't always have the capacity of adding water to their gardens. Thus, sand or white gravel is used as a substitute for water and this is why "dry landscape gardens" (Karesansui) are very popular. Lines formed when raking the sand can depict the flow of rivers and streams but usually a larger mass of water – a sea.

Natural Plants

In some Japanese gardens, the form of plantings is considered much more important than bright colours. In Kyoto the Shoden-Ji Garden has replaced rocks with mounds of pruned and clipped Azaleas, which rarely flower because of their constant shaping within the garden. This is in itself an art form but you should be aware that if you choose to include plants,trees or shrubs there will be an element of regular care.

The flowers and plants chosen to accompany a Zen Garden should be suitable for the climate that the garden is subject to. The available landscape within the garden space should also be estimated and taken into consideration. Additionally, planting soil will also have to match the plants requirements. A small amount of gravel or sand at the bottom of the planting hole will assist with the correct drainage.

One thing that you may have noticed about Zen or 'Dry' gardens is the topiary involved. This is not as daunting as it may first seem. For example, carefully clipped Azaleas placed together with surrounding gravel or sand would make an attractive "distant view" of a range of hills if placed correctly.

Smaller plants will take a much longer time to grow so a good idea to achieve swifter results is to buy slightly larger plants. Different sizes and shapes mean visual variation and add to the natural appearance of the garden.

Ornaments

Ornaments are often used to decorate Zen Gardens usually in the form of lanterns and statues (mainly Buddha representations).

Lanterns essentially offer Yang to reduce the dominance of Yin. These two polarities united serve as the perfect state of harmony. Yang balances Yin and vice versa. Yang, in this case the lantern element, becomes the white circle in the black; the fire to shield from the cold; the life to enlighten and vitalise from the dark. It offers the perfect essence of a Yang in a Yin environment. The lantern represents the gardens realisation of time, night and day, year after year. It transcends time and its physical structure and design perfectly attune to the climate of Japan by offering a hood for the snow and ice and a roof and walls to protect a candles flame. The lantern can sit beside a pond, in the pond, within a corner of the garden, alongside a pathway. It's best not located where the "sha" (detrimental) energy can extinguish it e.g., exposed on a hill in a gully or swamp, where the constant damp will extinguish the flame, or if used in a low place lifted above it on a pedestal to become a beacon similar to a lighthouse on a seashore guiding ships at sea.

Buddhas in Zen gardens are popular elements, as Japanese gardening has a close association with Buddhism. In a Japanese garden the soil represents the fertile mind of Buddha and our own internal Karma. Planting is interpreted as blossoming ideas from fertility. Paths signify the way to enlightenment. Zen Buddhism teaches that making a garden encourages contentment and enlightenment. This is the reason that in more recent times within the context of Japanese garden history, gardening is considered a spiritual and religious activity.

The general rules of thumb for placing Buddha statues in a Zen garden (or a Japanese garden) is facing north. South facing is not recommended as it is related to Yama a Hindu god and select in the dead. The Buddah statue is usually placed in a Lotus pool.

Moss

Moss may not always be included in a Zen Garden, yet quite a few seem to embrace its use. Grasses, perennial plants, bamboo and ivy will usually accompany moss, forming a stunning motif of contrasting earthy colours. The Silver Temple in Kyoto is a stunning example of a mossy Zen Garden. The western part of Kyoto is also filled with moss-adorned gardens, the most striking of all being the Saiboji Temple or "Moss Temple". Ninety different types of mosses are incorporated in the garden.

Moss, however, is generally difficult to cultivate and comes in various forms and sizes. It requires far less maintenance than grasses but is very particular on where it likes to grow; areas populated with weeds and general debris like decaying leaves are simply out of the question, as they interfere with its growth. Shaded and semi-shaded areas of a garden space on the other hand are best because they retain moisture for most varieties of moss.

Moss is resilient to both cold and damp weather, as it exploits any nutrients that may surround it. These nutrients are usually absorbed through its leaves, which simultaneously absorb moisture – this is the reason they cannot be covered for growth.

Types of Moss:

Rock Cap Moss (Dicranum): This type of moss loves deeply shaded areas and is perfect for stones and rocks in a Zen Garden.

Cushion Moss (Leukobryum Glacum): This variety has a slight sun tolerance but requires a predominantly sandy soil. It is usually light green in colour with silvery flecks.

Hair Cap Moss (Polythirchum Commune): This kind grows in a medium-shaded area and can be placed in partial sunlight. It loves sandy and acidic soil.

Moss can be transplanted to your garden and encouraged to

grow, but be solicitous in choosing the appropriate type to suit your garden. Moss is estimated to be hundreds of millions of years old as a species and knows what it wants and can stop growing when conditions are not favourable. Simply restart its growth when things take a turn for the better.

A little tip for fresh, relatively quick-growing moss is to coat your stones with "clean" natural yoghurt and watch them over a relatively short space of time turn green. Moss tends to grow abundantly in the right habitat and all that is required on your behalf is to provide moisture and patience.

Shortly, we will move on to the construction of my own Zen garden step by step and, as you will see, I have chosen to keep a line of natural rocks on one side of the garden, some of which have natural moss growth.

MAKING YOUR OWN ZEN GARDEN:
WHAT YOU NEED TO KNOW

So you may have decided to make your own Zen Garden or been thinking about it. Here are some factors and important points to consider before you go ahead with your garden?

1. Have you got enough space for a Zen Garden? If so, is this space exterior or interior? How big a space do you reasonably have available?

2. Are you fully aware and up to speed on the ingredients needed for your garden design?

3. Is your budget sufficient for the creation and care of your Zen Garden? This can massively vary depending on your plan and ambitions.

4. Have you got enough time to plan, build and maintain your garden?

5. What will the purpose of your Zen Garden be? Will it be there for meditation purposes or will it simply be decorative?

6. What type of Zen Garden do you want to make (dry landscape, courtyard, flat, etc)?

7. Does the style of the Zen Garden you have chosen to create correspond to the ingredients, space and design you are keen to implement?

8. Have you decided on whether you plan to do-it-yourself as a project or would you prefer to enlist the help of professional Japanese garden landscapers?

9. Will you be using water or dry water (sand or gravel)? Have you the facilities, tools and ingredients for the first option?

10. Are you keen on Feng Shui philosophy for your garden? Or are you randomly picking a space for it?

11. Have you pinpointed what plants you would like to use? Are you sure these plants can be utilized in the area your garden in situated in? Interior/ or exterior? And what about plants that are already part of the natural surroundings?
12. Will you garden be exposed to pets and visitors? The last thing you want is for your lovely pet to use your new garden as a giant litter tray!
13. Will your Zen Garden have a traditional or more modern appeal to it?
14. Will you be using ornaments? Which ones and where will they be placed?

Questions like these are supposed to pile up before plunging into creating a Zen Garden. It's not as though you can simply re-plant, re-fix and re-place anything that may not seem right, as you would in a regular garden – Zen Gardens adhere to certain philosophy of space and size and any attempt to "patch up" what may have gone wrong, is a product of exaggerative Western mentality which in no way corresponds to minimalistic Zen Gardens. Every element in a Zen Garden has its own specific position, direction size and meaning - make sure you understand and have made firm decisions- before grabbing the shovel.

Who Makes a Japanese Zen Garden Nowadays?

Japanese Zen Gardens bring peace, serenity and tranquillity to any outside or inside space if chosen well. But what makes these gardens so enticing and easily-adopted by Westerner's is the fact that they are as convenient as they are mind-easing. Just think of a beautiful courtyard garden on your rooftop, or a small dry landscape garden through the hallway of your house or office. Even the most confined of spaces can facilitate a small or miniature Zen Garden.

There was recently a story about a person who created a Zen garden in an egg shell, so size is really immaterial to your project it is just what you are comfortable with.

No matter who you are, what you know about gardening and how elaborate your background knowledge on plants is, you have to start at point zero when making a Japanese Zen Garden. This is why the process is fun as well as educating – not to mention that you are left with a serenely stunning garden for an end product.

When making a Japanese Zen garden you should use the elements in nature that you already have or are provided with and, with a little knowledge, you can design your space and arrange the constituents to reflect the peaceful feeling that you desire. And while there is a lot of work entailed to the creation of even the smallest of gardens, the result is its own reward.

Some More Things to Understand about Japanese Zen Gardens

Japanese philosophy reasons that everything OLD has a value. This applies to when you are making a Japanese Zen garden. Boulders overgrown with moss, old trees, stone arrangements are all examples of this mantra.

Nature in a Zen garden is fundamental and its appearance should reflect natural looks rather than a manufactured appearance – even if the garden is designed in a specific way and by definition is not old at all. Perennials and bulbs are sporadically planted to highlight the natural character of the garden rocks that are placed "naturally" in the design itself. Stone and water go together in a Zen garden and the water element can be anything from a shallow stone basin through to a pond or even a small waterfall. Water is something that you will realise is not only essential for a lot of people but is also relaxing and pleasing on the senses.

Japanese Zen gardens always stress the importance of the proportionate beauty of nature itself. They can be very time-consuming to look after if you opt for a large scale garden with a fair amount of foliage but that is part of the dedication you will need to be a Japanese Zen gardener. All Japanese gardens are designed to hide any form of human interference and to display a "natural world".

At the end of the day you can do whatever you wish with your Japanese Zen garden design but, assuming you have an interest in this unique form of gardening, following the guidelines is what you need to do!

The Importance of Edging

In a Japanese garden and its design principles you will often hear about 'flow'. A Japanese garden has to be something with a clean and crisp visual appearance and 'flow' – this is so everything appears to naturally follow on in the viewers' eyes. Think of it as 'visual tidiness'.

Edging is used in all sort of gardens all over the world but in a Japanese garden , when placed properly and with the right materials, it can really be highly effective. You could have a borderline between the garden and other parts of your space if you are just utilising a small area. A borderline can also be used to give paths an edge too.

In a Japanese garden you can use all sorts of edging materials. Cast stone, Bamboo, edging stones, slate, bricks and even an iron fence.

Slate because of its different shades will provide clean lines in your project when making a Japanese garden. Terracotta is also one of the top edging ingredients used because of its shade of colour. Stone can be used for edging a pond or a smaller building.

In a Japanese garden, gravel can be used as either a pathway OR as a border to give a distinguishing line between areas. The use of bricks is becoming more common in Japanese garden design and not as a straight line laid out going one way or another. Bricks can be laid in all sorts of ways to make the garden interesting – so do not be afraid to experiment.

Concrete can be moulded easily for any kind of edging look that you want to achieve. River rock gives a totally natural feel to edging and cast stone is sometimes used as an alternative for natural rock.

Edging with bamboo is a way of creating some intricate edging for the garden. Simply, cut the cane of the bamboo to the height that you want and bury in the ground for quick and effective results. Sometimes, metal fencing is added to Japanese gardens as some people feel that its addition adds a certain amount of elegance.

Japanese gardens are renowned for their peace and tranquillity, so remember the colour and style of the edging that you choose NEEDS to match and follow the natural flow of the garden. A couple of good tips – a Japanese garden is all about nature, so if you do some edging with rocks don't make them all the same size because in nature that simply wouldn't happen. Spread the rocks around in different sizes. The same goes with trees or shrubs – think NATURAL in your design thoughts and you should find that the ideas flow quickly and naturally for your design.

SUMI (BALANCE) IN ZEN GARDENS

In Japanese gardens "Sumi" or balance is very important and it is the reason why they are the way that they are. Balance refers to the gardens relationship with nature.

For example you would not put a square pond in a Japanese garden as perfectly square ponds do not exist naturally in nature. The same can be said of fountains – they are manmade, so a better option would be a natural waterfall or even a meandering stream.

Most Japanese Zen gardens are designed to recreate large landscapes but in much smaller forms – even if you only have a tiny space for making your garden. The smaller the space, the more thought you should give to your gardens design and ingredients as you have less space to play with. In a small space there is no point putting an imposing waterfall or very large rocks and stones. The balance of the garden will be completely wrong and will be obvious to the eye.

Here is a typical example of how elements of the garden "mirror" real landscapes. Rocks would be mountains and ponds would be lakes. "Dry water" or sand – which is raked for a water effect - would depict an ocean or large body of water. Stones can be placed on the sand for an "island" effect.

In a Japanese Zen garden you MUST embrace nature and aim to keep things in your garden as natural as possible. Minimalism is an important concept when making a Japanese garden. LESS really is MORE. Remember that phrase and it will help you get the right garden balance. If you remember ONE thing about Zen gardening, it should be that principle.

Don't be afraid to leave empty spaces in your Zen garden – it's a concept that is alien to western gardens but is very noticeable when you visit or look at images of Japanese gardens. Space or "Ma" is one of the gardens ingredients!

Japanese gardeners will set up their garden space for each season including winter. In fact, winter and spring are the two most important seasons in Japanese gardens – snow on branches is called snow blossom or "Sekku", snow on a lantern is an iconic image of a winter in a Japanese garden. Japanese gardens celebrate the cycle of life and death, which is reflected in the turn of seasons. When creating a Zen Garden, always plan for the garden to reflect each season and don't just let it die in late autumn and winter. If you are choosing not to have plants and shrubs, your job is made that much easier.

BUILDING A SMALL ZEN GARDEN

SMALL SPACE GARDENS

"Small is beautiful" - that is what some people say and in the case of *making a Japanese Zen garden* it is particularly true. *Small* Zen gardens are ideal if you have limited space or a roof terrace or balcony area. They can be built indoors as well as outdoors, in fact some of the smaller Zen gardens I have seen are the most beautiful.

There is no doubt that when you build a Japanese Zen garden you are copying the style and ideals that a native garden in Japan consists of and by definition you will not achieve the same "spiritual" feeling. A Western persons understanding of the cultural and spiritual importance of Japanese gardens and Zen Gardens is limited unless your read this publication!!.

Small Zen Gardens usually do not incorporate water, especially if they are interior gardens but that is not to say that you cannot be a little ambitious if you wish. Dry Landscape and Courtyard gardens are often the easiest designs to "shrink" into a smaller area.

To make a small Japanese garden you will need some or all of the following depending on your chosen style:

- plants
- rocks
- a lantern or stone basin
- some sand/ or gravel
- an open space or enclosed area.

Believe it or not, according to the strict rules of Japanese Zen gardens, even putting 2 rocks in a small enclosed area can be considered a garden! Kyoto is one of the main centres of Japanese gardening and it is accepted as the home of these types of gardens, which in Japanese are called "tsuboniwa".

In this area of Japan, maples, rocks, basins, fences, sand and plants and trees come together. Lilacs are used as are camellia and daphne.

Don't be put off by these rules – you can bend them and make your own landscape scene when making a Zen garden, the choice is yours but if it is authenticity you would like then copying a landscape in miniature is the way to go.

Location Ideas:

- on a rooftop terrace
- in a small office corner or reception area
- on an apartment balcony
- across a wide hallway
- in a living area
- in or next to a larger garden space
- by a swimming pool
- on a porch / veranda
- in a small wooden box for a table top

STEPS TO CREATING A SMALL SPACE GARDEN

STEP 1. Take a look at the various possible areas where you feel you could locate your Zen garden. Consider the positive and negative aspects of each spot.

You will need a quite area with little noise pollution from neighbours or busy roads. For my Zen garden I chose an area of my rear garden/yard that was secluded and had enough space to compliment its surroundings and be aesthetically pleasing to look at once built.

STEP 2. It is really helpful to help you focus on your new Zen garden to measure out and draw a SCALE plan on a piece of paper. Nothing too fancy just lay out the dimensions and how you expect it to look in terms of edges, contents and elements such as stones. Below is an image of my rough sketch – Michelangelo I am not! – but, you get the idea. A good scale to use is 1inch to 1 foot or if you want to make your plan bigger you can increase it to 2 inches to 1 foot if you wish.

You will see that I have drawn the shape and ingredients for my simple Zen garden , so I have a clear idea of what it will look like after construction. Play around with your design until you reach a point where you are satisfied with everything within the garden.

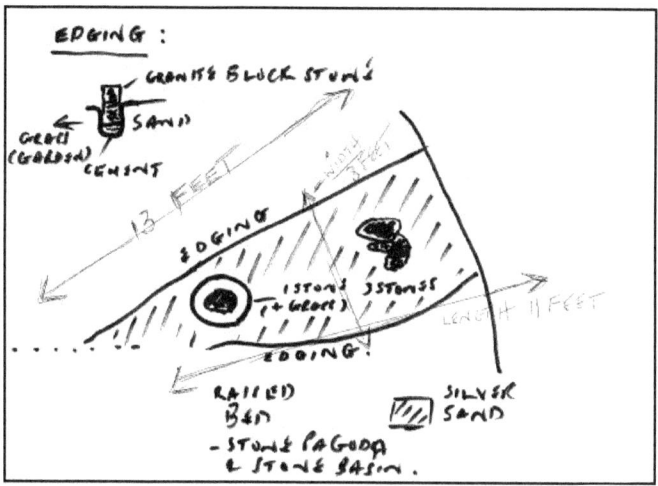

STEP 3. You need to dig out the area if it is grassy like mine. I dug to a depth of approx 4 inches and although the sides are not entirely straight (see below) they will be in the finished garden.

When digging out try and ensure you get rid of large stones and weeds or they will come back to haunt you later on. So, a little extra time spent doing this will get you the best results. You can also spray the area with a strong weed killer to help in this.

STEP 4. Next, it's the `EDGING´ that needs to be done. Edging comes in multiple varieties. It can be wooden planks, stone slabs or in my case small blocks of a type of granite called ´Storm´ these types of edging blocks are available from any garden centre or Home depot as well as specialist aggregate suppliers all over the world.

You need to measure the exactly lengths of the sides of your garden and work out how much edging you will need. For my garden the cost of the blocks was around 80 Pounds Sterling or approx 110 US Dollars. Brush your edging before setting in concrete to get rid of any impurities, then you are ready to position it around the garden area.

Be generous with your concrete as it has to hold the edging and within the garden quite a weight of sand or gravel. Tip: do NOT attempt to concrete edging if rain is in the weather forecast as it will struggle to set and you will have to go back to square one. Try and wait for a couple of dry days for the best results.

STEP 5. The next step is to complete all the edging and 'point' with cement between every edging block – the same applies if you are using lengthier blocks of stone or larger slabs. The cement has to be stronger than that used for brickwork in a house which tends to crumble over time when exposed to the elements. When you have completed the relatively time-consuming pointing, you can then place your weed suppressant mat within the confines of the garden. The matting comes in rolls and I had plenty left over for my next garden!! The cost was 35 Pounds Sterling or Approx 50 US Dollars.

The mat should be secured tightly and as snugly as possible to try and ensure that you do not get unwanted weeds constantly appearing through your Zen garden sand or gravel. Put the effort in to ensure future rewards, this part of your construction is not one for short cuts.

STEP 6. You will have made up your mind about the elements that you want placed in your Zen garden. I chose stones and did not really want any plants or shrubs within the Zen garden confines. You will see that I chose an area behind the Zen garden where I can locate a Stone basin, have my Buddha statue and greenery as well as an Acer Pallatum (very common in Japanese gardens). I may add some Bamboo grass at a later date but that would be it. Less is MORE.

I placed the stones in groupings of 3 and 1 (odd numbers) on my mat to check whether the placements on my original plan actually looked suitable.

Then you have two choices, either you can tightly cut your weed suppressant mat to exactly fir the shape of the bottom of each stone or if you are satisfied that your mat will stop any weed growth you can  simply place them in position. My ultimate plan is to have the smaller single placement stone surrounded by a circle of lush grass to signify and island – this requires quite a lot of work to get right and instructions on how to do it and pictures to help you do the same will feature in the next issue of this publication.

To get my stones I visited a local specialist supplier and chose them for their smoothness. I did not want very large stones but you may want them. Always try and view a variety of stones and types before buying and try to do it in person and not by buying online. Stones have a character all of their own and you will connect more with certain shapes and sizes. The cost of the stones that I got for my garden was once again very reasonable at around 45 Pounds Sterling or approximately 65 US Dollars.

STEP 7. Sand or Gravel? I opted for a type of sand called 'Silver' sand , once again sourced from an builders merchant. I chose it because of the colour and for easier and more effective raking. A lot of Zen gardens use gravel instead of sand and obviously it is a matter of personal preference. The sand needed for my Zen garden was approximately 1 metric tonne and the cost was 85 Pounds Sterling approx 110 US Dollars. Not overly expensive.

With the edging done, the mat in and the stones in place in went the Silver sand.

I will put soil and other small rocks or gravel in the gaps between the grass and the sloped areas to put the final touches to the gardens exterior borders.

Apart from the island construction in the future I sourced a small stone lantern that is not quite in a colour to match the garden's colours so I will be sanding that down and putting an oil based undercoat on it (important to hold any future coloured paint correctly) and that will be placed in one of the corners.

The great thing about designing a Zen garden is that you can let your mind wander and decide on ingredients to add once your basic design and construction is complete.

I now have a garden in the space that I wanted and as you can see in the image below it is ready for raking and the final touches to be done! It is 13 feet long and 3 and a half feet wide and cost in total around 450 Pounds Sterling to make which is approximately 600 US Dollars. There was a little heavy work and I did use a skilled workman to do the edging concreting and pointing in between the blocks. You may be confident enough to do it your self but remember concrete goes hard quickly and is difficult to take up and start your construction again.

Your budget will determine what ingredients and what quality you buy. Personally I recommend not buying because things are cheap but to always go for quality ingredients in a Zen garden and in a more ambitious 'Courtyard' garden.

Making a Japanese Courtyard Garden

In Japan, Courtyard Gardens were built with space at a premium and for somewhere to go and sit in peace to get away from searing summer heat. They are never big gardens and would be a perfect consideration for you if you are limited for space.

Copyright Cathy Cawood 2012-08-04

Quality design, ideas and materials are essential to give a courtyard garden the right look, feel and ambience. Sometimes they can just be a place to de-stress and relax and some are built for wellbeing purposes.

A 'courtyard' garden in Japanese is Tsuboniwa and essentially is an enclosed garden space and despite the lack of space they take up it gives you a really good opportunity to express yourself and your design ideas. Remember this is a garden project that is small and viewed close up which means it will need to be of a high quality.

Whether you want it for tranquillity or as a wellness garden, your design needs to be well thought through and there are a number of ingredients to think about. Stones and rocks in Japanese gardens as you may know play a very important role and so they do in a courtyard garden.

Making a Japanese garden is the dream of many people all over the world and this small enclosed variety can look stunning with a little effort. Here's what you should look at using:

- Gravel
- Plants
- Stones (perhaps the most important ingredient)

- Ornaments and other objects can also be used, such as a basin (Chozubachi), hand washing utility (Tsukubai), stone lantern(s) (Toro), stepping stones as part of a water feature (Tobishi), stone paving (nobedans).

A Japanese garden uses rocks and stones as a focal point for the viewer or visitor and it's the same when making a Japanese Courtyard Garden. Quality of design and ingredients should be your watchword.

Courtyard Garden Essentials

So what are the elements you can use when making a Japanese garden? If you wish to be accurate and traditional then a stone basin is a must, stone pathways, a lantern, maybe a small bridge and some garden stones. These are all strong elements and are often referred to by designers as 'hardscape'.

Hardscape will help you set out and realise your design ideas. For example you could place a small bridge over an area of sand or gravel (depicting water) or you could place a few larger stones within your design that would mimic real landscapes like mountains.

Plants, shrubs and herbaceous trees will complete the finished design. As always, my advice is to sketch out your designs before starting the construction. A good rule of thumb is one inch squared equals one square foot on your plan.

It is quite possible that your Japanese courtyard garden will have walls on each side and may be denied generous sunlight so you will have to pick your trees, shrubs and plants accordingly. If it is a really shady are then go for mosses – they will flourish and provide a blanket of different greens and the occasionally light brown to accentuate your hardscape features.

Your sunlight in the garden will dictate what plants and shrubs will flourish in an area of direct sunlight, shade or bright light (not direct sunlight).It's a small scale garden so try and stick with dwarf bonsai and a good dollop of groundcover plants that fit your environment. Always check the growing needs before buying to avoid disappointment.

The chances are your Japanese courtyard garden will not be blessed with lots of natural water so pick plants that require little water. If you feel uncomfortable about including plants, shrubs and bonsai trees then you can always just design a space that is a traditional 'Tsuboniwa'. By this I mean DRY

– no water or plants etc. The earliest and more traditional courtyard gardens follow this 'rule'.

They used rocks, sand, gravel etc to copy real landscapes scenes from a familiar local area. It is fun using your imagination – rake sand in swirls to signify water, a stone basin containing water can signify a lake or even an ocean! You can go small medium or large with your landscape copying, it will depend on the size of your available area.

A Japanese courtyard garden takes some organising and thought. Don't just place ingredients willy-nilly. Your plan should reflect an area of contemplation, tranquillity and spiritual learning and reflection. Do not overcrowd it!

I heard a saying that is SO true ..." Plan your Japanese courtyard garden with a minimalist approach and the economy of a poet"

www.ingramcontent.com/pod-product-compliance
Lightning Source LLC
Chambersburg PA
CBHW071322080526
44587CB00018B/3327